# CHRISTOPHER COLUMBUS

## To the New World

## James Lincoln Collier

**Marshall Cavendish**
Benchmark
New York

Marshall Cavendish Benchmark
99 White Plains Road
Tarrytown, NY 10591-9001
www.marshallcavendish.us

Library of Congress Cataloging-in-Publication Data
Collier, James Lincoln, 1928-
Christopher Columbus : to the New World / by James Lincoln Collier.
p. cm. — (Great explorations)
Summary: "An exploration of the life and momentous voyages of the
Italian-born explorer"—Provided by publisher.
Includes bibliographical references and index.
ISBN-13: 978-0-7614-2221-1
ISBN-10: 0-7614-2221-8
1. Columbus, Christopher—Juvenile literature. 2.
Explorers—America—Biography—Juvenile literature. 3.
Explorers—Spain—Biography—Juvenile literature. 4. America—Discovery and
exploration—Spanish—Juvenile literature. I. Title. II. Series.

E111.C6195 2007
970.01'5092—dc22

2006001461

Photo research by Anne Burns Images

Cover photo: Corbis/Bettman
Cover inset: Granger Collection

The photographs in this book are used by permission and through the courtesy of:
*Granger Collection:* 5, 7, 8, 16, 19, 21, 24, 25, 40, 42, 43, 63, 64. *Corbis:* Leonard de Selva, 10;
Michael S. Yamashita, 11; Corbis, 15; Brooklyn Museum of Art, 31; Archivo Iconografico, S.A., 35;
Bettman, 38; Maps.com, 68; Julio Donoso/Sygma, 70; Michael Appleton, 74. *North Wind Picture
Archive:* 22, 29, 32, 45, 48, 53, 59, 61. *Bridgeman Art Library:* Prado, 47; Giraudon, 54;
Johnny van Haeften Gallery, 56. *Art Resource:* Erich Lessing, 58; Scala, 67, 72.

Printed in China
1 3 5 6 4 2

# Contents

# O N E

# A Young Man finds His Way

Christopher Columbus is one of the most famous men in world history. Indeed there are some people who believe he is the most famous of all. It is an arguable point; but there is no doubt that what he did in the space of a few years changed history forever. Without Columbus, the world we are living in would be quite different from what it is.

Still, Columbus is well known mostly for the wrong reasons. If you asked people what Columbus did that was important, many would say that he set out to prove the world was round by sailing west to "the Indies," instead of going east as Europeans had always done, and by chance bumped into America. There is a little truth to this story but not much as will become evident when his life and accomplishments are more closely examined.

We know a great deal less about Columbus and his voyages than we would like to. Famous during his life, within a few decades of his

4

Although this portrait of Columbus was made after his death, it is considered to be the best likeness that we have.

death in 1506, he was almost completely forgotten. As a result, nobody thought to take proper care of the many reports, diaries, and letters he wrote describing his four trips to the New World. Not for several centuries did anyone bother to study his life, and by that time most of what he had written was gone.

Luckily some of his letters remain. There are also some court documents and legal papers about him still in existence. Most important, a few people who knew him or saw his reports and diaries wrote their own versions of what they had learned about Columbus. It is from the writings of these people that most of our knowledge of Columbus comes.

Columbus himself was also partly responsible for our inability to know him as we should. He was, if nothing, a proud man, even arrogant in his later years. He did not want people to know about his humble upbringing, and as he grew famous in his day, he tried to keep quiet about his family and childhood.

This much we know. Columbus was born in 1451 in the port city of Genoa, an important seafaring city in the northwestern part of what is now Italy. His father, Domenico Colombo (the Italian version of Columbus), was a weaver. His mother, Susanna, was the daughter of a weaver. His father may have been at one time or another a tavern keeper and a guardian of one of the city's gates, although that is not certain. He had a younger sister and two younger brothers. He remained close to his brothers who sometimes helped him in his explorations.

In the normal course of things, Columbus would have grown up to be a weaver, the family trade. But it is clear that even in his youth Columbus was determined to rise above his origins. This need to be known, to be seen as important, drove him throughout his life. We sometimes talk about the "forces of history" as shaping patterns of life; but it is also true that the characters of human beings have their effect, too. Without Columbus's determination to accomplish great deeds, the history of the past five hundred years would have been much different.

In Columbus's time, one of the best ways to rise in the world was by volunteering to fight for one of the many powerful lords who controlled often vast parcels of land. Here heavily armored knights set out to do battle.

---

In Renaissance Europe, in order to advance, one usually needed the support and sponsorship of a wealthy or powerful person. Ambitious young men usually got ahead by joining the powerful and wealthy Roman Catholic Church or by fighting in the army of one of the many

Making his mark—a sample of Columbus's handwriting. The ability to read and write were valuable skills not to be taken for granted.

dukes, princes, and kings who controlled their own private portions of the European landscape.

But changes were taking place in Europe that were opening up a new way for ambitious young men to advance in life. Before about 1100 or 1200, the continent lacked the technological and cultural sophistication of China and the Muslim empire, which stretched through the Near East, across North Africa, and into Portugal and Spain. It was Muslim philosophers and writers, not European ones, who kept interest in the Greek thinkers, like Aristotle, alive.

Then, for reasons historians still debate, Europeans began making strides. Starting in the twelfth century, Europeans began to advance in art, literature, and philosophy. They also developed clocks, gunpowder-based weapons, and better ways of working with glass and metals. Along with sudden advancements in technology, trade, what is today called business, was becoming of key importance to Europeans. Small factories were started for making glassware, guns, armor, cloth, and much else. All over Europe traders were buying and selling. A trader might buy wool from investors in England, which he could sell to the weavers of Flanders, a region that included parts of what are today northern France, Belgium, and the southwestern Netherlands. He might also buy cloth from Flanders to sell to merchants in Venice; or buy glass from Venetian brokers to sell in London.

All of this commerce was heavily dependent on boats and ships. The roads of Europe were generally in poor condition, and there were high mountains and many rivers to cross. It was much easier and safer to ship goods from, for example, Venice to Lisbon by water, even though the land route was shorter. As a result, European ships improved steadily, and European sailors grew more daring and accomplished.

By Columbus's times all of this activity in commerce, the arts, and technology had reached a peak known as the Renaissance. Our modern world, historians believe, came out of the Renaissance. Even as Columbus was plotting the voyages that would make him famous, artists such as Michelangelo and Leonardo da Vinci were painting their master-pieces, the great Greek and Roman writers of a thousand or more years earlier were being rediscovered. Thinkers such as Erasmus were creating works still quoted today. It was a productive time of great activity.

For traders, an area that held great interest was *the East*. This term was used to cover a then mysterious part of the world we know today as India, China, Japan and the adjoining lands, especially those islands that make up Indonesia. Only a handful of Europeans had ever visited the mysterious East. One, Marco Polo, had written a famous book

The creation of the modern university was important to the advance of Europe as a major cultural presence in the world. Universities encouraged the increase and spread of knowledge. One of the earliest ones was the University of Paris, shown here.

Marco Polo, one of the first Europeans to travel extensively in China, wrote a celebrated report of what he had seen that suggested there was great wealth to be had in the East.

about his travels there, but European knowledge of the area was thin.

However, for centuries certain kinds of trade goods had been entering Europe from the East, sometimes just a trickle, sometimes a steady flow. Precious goods like silk, gold, pearls, jade, ivory, and spices brought enormous prices in Europe. A trader who could get hold of even a small amount of such goods could sell them for a fortune.

These goods were not being shipped across the seas, however, but over the so-called Silk Road, which is the name given to the various routes that wound out of China and across what is now central Asia, usually entering Europe through Istanbul (then called Constantinople) and the eastern Mediterranean. It was a dangerous trip, for all along the several thousand miles of the route there were bandits who preyed on the caravans, as well as rivers and mountains to cross or skirt.

# THE LURE OF THE EAST

In Columbus's time, some of the most valuable products available to Europeans came from the so-called East—the lands now known as India, China, Japan, Malaysia, and the various nearby islands. These included pearls, silks, and exotic woods like mahogany, which did not grow in Europe. But most important of all were spices—pepper, cinnamon, cloves, ginger, cardamom, turmeric, nutmeg, mace, and more. Today such spices are commonplace, but in fifteenth-century Europe they were of great value and the demand was high. Europeans had few good systems for preserving food. Meat especially was often partially spoiled by the time it came to the table. Vegetables that were out of season would grow rancid in storage. It was believed that strong spices, especially pepper, helped to purify spoiled food. In any case, spices certainly disguised the smell of spoiling food. And they added a pleasant flavor to any number of dishes.

By the time of the ancient civilizations of Greece and Rome, spices were coming into Europe from the East via sea and land routes, many of which passed near or through what we now call the Middle East. The Arabs thus controlled much of the spice trade and forced prices up. The rise of Islam during the seventh century gave the Arabs control of huge swaths of land reaching from China to Spain, and their hold on trade from the East grew. In Europe, spices became increasingly scarce and more costly.

Between Arab control of important spice routes and the bandits who preyed on the spice caravans crossing the long expanses of hostile or contested land that stretched between the East and Europe, spices were hard to obtain. Thus a feverish search for a safe sea route from Europe to the East began. Columbus's voyages westward, toward what he hoped were the Indies, were driven in part by the high price in Europe of pepper, nutmeg, cloves, and ginger.

Europeans' understanding of the geography of the East, or the Indies as it was usually called, was sketchy indeed. A few maps had been drawn, but there were mainly guesswork. However, by the early 1400s, European knowledge of the Indies was improving. Particularly important was a Portuguese nobleman known as Henry the Navigator, who was obsessed with expanding his knowledge of the world. Henry began sending ships farther and farther along the western coast of Africa. His explorers mapped the African coast and founded some trading posts there. They also explored the Atlantic islands of Madeira, the Azores, and Cape Verde, some of which Columbus would ultimately visit. In 1486 the celebrated seaman Bartholomew Diaz rounded the Cape of Good Hope, the southernmost point of Africa. He sailed from there across the Indian Ocean and into the Pacific.

When Diaz returned with his report, many concluded that they had found the route to the fabled Indies with its silk, jewels, gold, ivory, and other precious goods. Plans were made to send ships up the eastern coast of Africa to find—what exactly, nobody was sure.

But there were others who had different ideas. If you stand on shore and watch a tall ship sail out to sea, it would appear to grow smaller, as you would expect. But it will also appear to be sinking into the sea, so that in time only the top of the ship—the mast or funnels—will be visible. The early Greeks, who were good seamen, had noticed this. Their philosophers had also made a serious attempt at understanding the motions of the stars, planets, Moon, Sun, and Earth. From these initial investigations, some Greek thinkers concluded that the Earth was round—a sphere. Columbus, thus, had no need to "prove that the world was round." By the time he was born, the idea was accepted by scientists and many scholars.

To the educated, it was obvious that you could get to the fabulous wealth of the Indies by sailing west across the Atlantic that washed up on the beaches of parts of coastal Europe. The big question was, how

The Portuguese prince known as Henry the Navigator was, like many Europeans, fascinated by the strange, largely unknown lands of Africa and Asia. He studied navigation and encouraged explorers to set off for foreign places. As a result, Portugal became the first major European colonizing power.

Johann Gutenberg's printing of the Bible, shown here, triggered a great upsurge in book making. Knowledge spread much faster than before, and it became possible for people with little money to learn to read and be able to study the arts and sciences.

far across that empty stretch of water would a ship have to travel to reach Cipangu or Cathay, as Japan and China were then known? If it were only a few hundred miles, sailing west to the Indies might be possible; if it were much longer the Indies might not be reachable from that direction, for a ship could carry enough food and water to last sailors for only a certain number of days. Traveling east around Africa was different, for a ship moving along the coast could land to find supplies. But who knew what was out there in the Atlantic?

This, then, was the situation in Europe as Columbus was growing up. What precisely he was planning and thinking we do not know. However, it is clear enough that he was determined to improve himself. At the time, books were not easy for a poor boy to get hold of. Printing had only recently been developed, and while Europe would soon be flooded with books, in Columbus's youth they were still expensive.

He knew, however, that if he were to rise in life, he had to acquire knowledge. Somehow he learned to read. Possibly he was taught by Catholic friars who were everywhere in the life of the times. Nonetheless he was mainly self-taught, reading everything he could lay his hands on, but especially history and geography. He also picked up a smattering of languages, certainly at least Spanish and Portuguese and possibly some others. And somehow, by the time he was fourteen, he began traveling on the trading ships that were constantly moving around the Mediterranean, up the Atlantic to England and France, down the western coast of Africa.

These were, for a boy from Genoa, faraway places. He visited England, Ireland, France, Turkey, and some of the Atlantic islands. But his destiny would not be trade; it would be the great Atlantic Ocean.

# T W O

# An Obsession Begins to Grow

What, precisely, Christopher Columbus was doing on the various trading voyages he made we do not know. There is no evidence that he was commanding any ships or even working as a sailor. He may have been in charge of goods being shipped by a merchant—especially woolen cloth, about which he knew something. Possibly he was trading in goods himself. He may have traveled as a translator or aide of some kind to a merchant or a ship's captain. Historians simply do not know. But there is solid evidence that during these years he did a lot of traveling by ship, both on the Atlantic and the Mediterranean.

How, why, and when did his mind turn to the possibility of the westward trip to the Indies? This, too, we do not know. It was, however, a subject very much thought about in Europe. After all, millions of Europeans lived along the Atlantic and many earned their livings from it: it was simply there when they woke up in the morning. And what was out in it?

In Columbus's time, European merchants were becoming wealthy through trade. Most goods were carried by water, rather than on land. By 1465, when this picture was painted, merchant ships could travel long distances. Harbors full of ships were commonplace.

People had a lot of different answers to that question, all of them guesses. Some believed that the Atlantic must be scattered with islands, like the Canary and Cape Verde islands. Others believed that there was a sort of twin to Europe across the Atlantic, which they called the antipodes. But many believed that across that empty stretch of water lay Cipangu, Cathay, and the fabulous wealth of the Indies. Some maps of the Atlantic had been drawn based on travelers' spotty reports of these much-sought places. On one such map Japan lay just north of where Venezuela is found. The coast of China lay in North America east of the Mississippi River. India, Ceylon (today called Sri Lanka), and the islands of the Indies were placed off the western coast of South America.

These maps were of course very inaccurate, but they did show the lands of the east in more or less the right relationship to one another. Unfortunately, some put the Indies more than 10,000 miles (16,093 kilometers) closer to Spain and Portugal than they actually were.

It depended on how big you thought the world was, for one thing; and how large the lands of the East were. Thus, if the globe was relatively small, and the lands of the East were big, it was reasonable to guess that the Indies lay not too far across the Atlantic. But if the opposite was true, the Indies might be thousands of miles away—as, in fact, they were—too far for ships of the time to sail unless there were islands along the way where they could restock supplies of food and water.

During the time that Columbus was in his twenties and thirties, these questions were hotly debated by seamen, geographers, philosophers, scientists, and anyone interested in cashing in on the wealth that could be made from trade with the Indies. Columbus was a man of great intellectual curiosity, and he began to study the geography question intensely. He pored over maps, studied the ancient theories about the size of the Earth, and talked to sailors about the places they had been and what they had seen there. The whole question of what lay out there beyond the Atlantic was becoming an obsession with him.

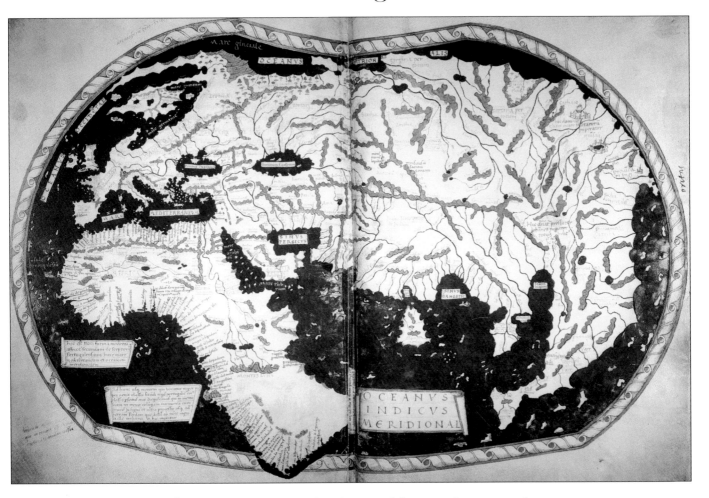

Maps of the time were rough. This world map, drawn in about 1489, is fairly accurate when it comes to Europe but grows increasingly incorrect with outlying regions and does not show the New World at all. China, Japan, and the neighboring islands have been crunched together. It is believed that Columbus had once consulted this map.

Columbus was by the 1470s and 1480s living in Lisbon, the capital of Portugal. It was a natural place for him to settle—a prosperous, seafaring nation at the forefront of European exploration. How he was making his living historians are once again not sure. There is some evidence that his studies of the Atlantic had led him into work as a bookseller and perhaps a mapmaker.

Through his research, he had come to believe that Japan and China were only several hundred miles out in the Atlantic—a reasonable distance for a ship of that time to travel. In truth, the evidence that the

This woodcut presents an artist's vision of Columbus studying maps in his studio.

Indies were much farther away was equally as credible. But it is important to note that Columbus was usually able to believe what he wanted and hoped to be true. If there had been questions in his mind about the distance to the Indies, he would not have attempted to sail there. But he had no doubts; he had made up his mind on that point.

When Columbus decided he was fated to make the great voyage we do not know. Probably the idea took shape slowly. If anyone could do it, why not he? He was, after all, a very ambitious man determined to make his mark. Anyone who found a route to the riches of the Indies could expect to become enormously wealthy. Furthermore, an explorer who discovered new lands, like the islands the Portuguese explorers had recently found, could claim them for his rulers. The rulers in turn would usually make the discoverer a sort of prince or ruler of the new lands. If Columbus could find a route to the Indies, he would become not only wealthy, but counted among the mighty.

To make such an exciting and frightening trip, Columbus needed money. He would need the support of a wealthy patron willing to gamble that Columbus would indeed reach the Indies and return with a shipful of gold, pearl, silks, and spices. The risks, of course, were high. Ships were regularly sunk by storms and attacked by pirates or the people of the islands where ships stopped for supplies. In this case, there was a good chance that the Indies were thousands of miles away, and that the sailors would die of thirst and hunger long before they got there.

But the backing of a wealthy patron was not by itself enough. In those days, citizens needed permission from their governments for any important undertaking. Columbus would need a nation behind him. At the moment the most likely possibilities were England, France, Spain, or Portugal. They all had ports on the Atlantic. They all were trying to build their sea trade. They all had fleets of merchant vessels and experienced sailors to man them. They all were run by powerful monarchs wealthy enough to support the venture.

Columbus first approached the king of Portugal. The king was interested but in the end, he turned Columbus down. It may have been that Columbus asked too much in return for doing the job—he would do that later in Spain as well. It may have been that the king's advisory committee did not believe that the venture was possible. It is also the case that the Portuguese felt that the best route to the East was around the southern tip of Africa and then north to India and China—as, in fact, it turned out to be. Whatever the case, the Portuguese king said no.

An etching made of Columbus in the nineteenth century. By then, American interest in Columbus was growing, and such pictures became popular.

A man obsessed does not easily give, may never give up. The idea that he could perform this magnificent deed, which would send his name echoing down the centuries, had gotten a grip on Columbus. He would not rest until it was done.

So he decided to try the rulers of Spain. There were two of them, and they would in time be enormously important to Christopher Columbus, as he would be to them. Today students first learn of Ferdinand and Isabella of Spain not as rulers of a powerful nation in the fifteenth century, but for the role they played in the life of Columbus.

At the time Columbus was born, Spain had been, like many other

An illumination from a 1492 manuscript showing Ferdinand and Isabella of Spain wearing elaborate court costumes and surrounded by their courtiers.

places, filled with quarrelsome counts and princes endlessly squabbling over who should rule what parts of the country. In 1469 two of these people, Ferdinand of Aragon and Isabella of Castille, were married, joining two of the major factions.

Both Ferdinand and Isabella were deeply religious. Ferdinand, who had grown up in a world where nobles were frequently disagreeing, had become devious. He would lie, or go back on promises, when he felt it necessary for him and for Spain. Isabella was more straightforward. But neither of them wanted their power challenged. They were, despite their religious natures, hard-headed monarchs who wanted things to go their way.

They were determined to achieve greatness for Spain, and they set about unifying their lands. One of their biggest problems was the people called the Moors. They were Muslims originally from North Africa, who some seven hundred years earlier had swept in Europe, taking over much of Spain and Portugal in the process. The Spanish eventually fought back and slowly drove the Muslims south. But by the time Columbus turned his eyes to Spain, the Moors still held the city of Granada and the surrounding territory. In the 1480s, the monarchs' greatest concern was not exploration, but ridding Spain of the Muslims.

Columbus knew that, but he could not see beyond his own proposed voyage. In 1485 he moved to Spain. A commoner like Columbus could not simply walk up to a king or queen and ask for favors, any more than an ordinary American citizen can get in to see the president. Fortunately Columbus was able to make a connection with the count of Medinaceli. This nobleman had long been involved in overseas trade, especially with the Canary Islands. He knew the promise of wealth such ventures offered, as well as the risks.

Columbus explained to the count his theories about the size of the world and how close he estimated the Indies were. The count was impressed. And indeed, Christopher Columbus was an impressive man. He was determined and had a natural way with words, as his writings reveal. Most important he had utter faith in his own scheme. That conviction came through in his voice and manner.

He ultimately convinced the count of Medinaceli. All he needed, he said, was three or four caravels, the type of ship frequently used by the

The kind of ship known as a caravel was popular in Columbus's day. Caravels usually had two or three masts and were lateen rigged, meaning a sail was hung from a long spar that could be tipped or shifted as necessary to take advantage of the wind. This picture is based on a drawing supposedly made by Columbus.

# THE MUSLIM PRESENCE

Following the death of Muhammad, the founder of Islam, in 632, the faith spread rapidly. The Arabs took Damascus in 635, Syria the following year, Jerusalem in 637, and in the same year swept through Iraq. Later, in 711, Muslim troops crossed the Strait of Gibraltar and began to conquer parts of Europe. Within twenty years they had claimed a large portion of Spain and Portugal.

Islam affected and influenced Spain in several ways. For one, the Muslims welcomed Jews and other peoples from North Africa into their lands. These groups went on to play important roles in Spanish government and society. For another, as anyone who has ever visited Spain knows, much of the older architecture has been deeply influenced by Muslim ideas of building and design. Such buildings as the Mesquita in Cordova, the Alhambra in Granada, and the Alcazar in Seville remain among Europe's finest architectural treasures.

Perhaps most important, in the years of the Muslim conquest the Arabs introduced their notions of mathematics, science, and philosophy to the region. While Europe lingered in the Dark Ages, the Arab world shone brightly. By about 1000 the tide turned and Europeans were starting to fight back. Slowly, various monarchs began to reclaim Muslim-held areas, and by 1250 they had reconquered all of Spain except for Granada, the heavily fortified town near the southern coast. The Muslim presence there gave the Arabs a base of power in Spain, a fact that annoyed Spanish rulers for more than two hundred years. Ferdinand and Isabella were determined to break the Muslim hold, succeeding in 1492 and thus opening the door for Columbus's famed voyages.

Spanish and the Portuguese for their voyages at the time. For the count, a small fleet of that size was not an impossible expense. He agreed to finance Columbus's trip. However, he knew that they could not go ahead without the permission of Ferdinand and Isabella. Because the count was a nobleman, he was known to the court. He wrote to the king and queen about Columbus, and they invited him to visit them.

In those days, things did not move with the swiftness and efficiency of modern times. Kings and queens did not make decisions in a hurry. Raising money for projects was often a slow process, and getting the men and material needed might be even slower. Important ventures often took years to get started. It would take Columbus six years to get his project going.

In 1486 he moved to Castile, where the court then resided. It was some time before he actually met with Ferdinand and Isabella. When he finally was able to tell them of his scheme, they seemed interested. Spain was lagging behind Portugal, its neighboring rival, in overseas exploration. Portugal had already established a trading base on the western coast of Africa and on the nearby island of Cape Verde. They were bringing back valuable goods, including gold and, regrettably, slaves.

The Spanish had done some exploring of their own and claimed the Canary Islands. Ferdinand and Isabella knew that the search for distant lands, while risky, might be enormously profitable. The Portuguese claimed rights to Africa, so Spain would have to look elsewhere. Perhaps out in the Atlantic there were islands filled with gold. Perhaps the legendary antipodes, laden with treasure, really did exist.

Most important, as Columbus insisted, it might be possible to reach the Indies by sailing west. The Indies were real, as were the precious goods that for centuries had come from the region. Ferdinand and Isabella decided the idea was worth considering. Late in 1486, a committee was put together to study Columbus's scheme. Early in 1487 the committee rejected the plan.

A painting showing Columbus pleading his case to Ferdinand and Isabella. The artist has given Columbus a commanding presence, which the explorer undoubtedly had.

Columbus, with his maps and globes, stands before the royal committee that was to pass judgment on the explorer's proposed voyage. Columbus was trying to prove that the Indies were closer to Europe than they actually were.

The committee members have often been seen as fools who spurned a genius, but in fact, there were several valid reasons for having doubts about the plan. Others who had studied the question believed that the world was much larger than Columbus claimed it was and that the Indies were much farther away than Columbus's calculations showed. (As it turned out, they were right.) Reasonable people might well conclude that the venture Columbus planned was far too risky to waste good money on. There was another consideration. The war against the Moors was costing a lot of money. There was little to spare for risky explorations.

Columbus had now been turned down by the rulers of Portugal and Spain. The rejections only made him more determined than ever. In 1488 he returned to Portugal, where he attempted once again to sway that nation's ruler. He got nowhere and went back to Spain. He had, by then, spent more than a year at the Spanish court. He had impressed many people there. Many of the courtiers who surrounded Ferdinand and Isabella were beginning to think that Columbus might actually be right. Perhaps the monarchs were missing a chance at great wealth.

Slowly the tide of opinion began to turn. Still, the monarchs could not be persuaded. The war with the Moors was their first priority. A year passed, then another, and another. Then in 1492, when Columbus was still with the Spanish court, the Moors in Granada surrendered. After seven hundred years, they had lost their foothold in Spain. The monarchs could turn their attention and their pocketbooks to other matters. Very quickly they decided to back Columbus's dangerous but potentially profitable scheme of reaching the Indies by sailing west.

# T H R E E

# The First Voyage

By 1492 Christopher Columbus had begun to believe that he was more than just another explorer looking for wealth. He was coming to see himself as a man with a great mission whom fate had entrusted with a magnificent task. His confidence and sense of self-importance compelled him to bargain with Ferdinand and Isabella almost as if he was their equal. If his trip was successful—and he had no doubt that it would be—he asked to be given the title Admiral of the Ocean Sea and viceroy of whatever lands he discovered. He also wanted, most of all, a share of the wealth that came from the new lands. It was a lot to demand, but Columbus had a way of getting people to respectfully listen to him, and the monarchs agreed to his terms. If Columbus's voyage was successful, he would come home not merely rich but a nobleman, the equal of the counts and dukes who surrounded him at the Spanish court.

Considering the amount of time it had taken to get permission for

This is one of the many portraits of Columbus made in the nineteenth century when a movement was under way to fully recognize the explorer's accomplishments. Note the globe and the ship's rigging in the background.

the trip, the venture got under way quickly. A key figure in setting it going was a man named Martín Alonso Pinzón. He was a ship owner who was based in the seaport town of Palos, not far from the border with Portugal. Pinzón was an important person in that area. He helped round up two ships, the *Nina* and the *Pinta*. Finding a crew was a different matter. A lot of the local sailors did not want to risk the trip, which seemed to them reckless, if not plain crazy. Of course they might become wealthy from it, but was that worth the risk? Pinzón persuaded many of them to take the chance. He would also serve as captain of one of the ships, the *Pinta*. Pinzón even saw himself as Columbus's partner in the venture, although Columbus certainly did not view the situation the same way.

Columbus got hold of a third ship, the *Santa Maria*, on which he

# COLUMBUS'S SHIPS

The *Nina*, *Pinta* and *Santa Maria* were caravels. These ships were small by today's standards. The largest of them, the *Santa Maria*, was about 85 feet (26 meters) long. Columbus's caravels had four sails. The most important, the mainsail, was attached to a mast taller than the ship's length. It did most of the driving.

Although the ships were short, they were relatively bulky and wide, both for greater stability and to increase carrying capacity. The hulls were colorfully painted above the waterline, and the sails were decorated with crosses and/or heraldic designs.

Such small ships could not carry large crews. The *Santa Maria* had forty men and boys aboard, the small *Nina* only twenty-one. Most of them were experienced sailors from the Palos area, but among them were three younger men, probably teenagers, who had been serving life sentences for helping a murderer escape from the law. They had been offered pardons in exchange for risking the trip with Columbus.

There was also in the group a man whose job it was to make sure that Ferdinand and Isabella got their share of the gold they expected Columbus to find. In addition, Columbus took along a man who could speak Arabic, with the hope that he would be able to communicate with the Japanese and Chinese they hoped to do business with.

Life on board was hard. The primary food for sailors, as it would be for centuries, was what we know as hardtack, teeth-breaking biscuits that over time became filled with maggots. Some sailors of the time made it a practice to eat their hardtack after dark, when they could not see the maggots.

An artist's vision of the Nina, Pinta, and the Santa Maria.
The lateen rigging of the sails was eventually replaced by better
systems, but it allowed a great deal of the canvas sail to catch the
maximum amount of wind. It proved to be an effective system,
in use for another hundred years.

would sail (it turned out to be the worst of the three vessels). He filled the ships with enough food and water for a long trip. He also took with him small bells, beads, and glass objects to trade for gold and spices with the people he expected to meet in the Indies. He chose these things because the Portuguese had been using them for trade in their African ventures. By the end of July, everything was arranged.

Columbus, to this point, had never been captain of a ship. But he had studied whatever he could about geography. He probably knew as much about winds and navigation as most sea captains, simply because so little was known about such matters at the time.

The first problem Columbus faced was the direction of the wind. A ship cannot sail directly into a head wind. It can, of course, sail with the wind behind it. It can also sail across the wind by setting the sail at the proper angle. In fact, it can sail at a fairly close angle into the wind, once again by managing the sail properly.

To sail directly into the wind, it is necessary to tack back and forth. The ship sails at an angle across the wind in one direction and then reverses course and sails in the opposite direction at an angle across the wind, moving in a zigzag pattern. Tacking, obviously, takes a lot longer than sailing with a favorable "following" or tailwind.

Because of the limited amount of food and water on board, Columbus needed to make the quickest voyage possible. That meant choosing a course that would give him the most favorable wind. Winds of course rise and fall, sometimes blowing with the fury of a hurricane, sometimes settling into a dead calm. But there is a general tendency for them to blow in certain predictable directions in various specific places on Earth. In the mid-Atlantic, winds tend to blow from east to west, or from Europe toward the United States. These are called the northwest trade winds, as winds are named for the direction they are coming from. Farther north are the westerlies, which blow, roughly, in the opposite direction.

By the time Columbus set out on his voyage, he had been sailing around the European side of the Atlantic for about twenty-five years. He had also spent hours talking to sailors about their experiences. Keeping this in mind, he chose for his first trip what would prove to be

This nineteenth-century engraving shows Columbus making the first sighting of land. There is considerable doubt that it was he who first saw the island, although he has often been given the credit.

almost exactly the best route for taking advantage of the most favorable winds. Over his four trips he would come to understand the Atlantic winds better, perhaps, than any seaman of his day.

A second problem was navigation, which was at the time more of an art than a science. The problem for a captain was to tell where the ship was in the middle of open water without any markers of any kind.

Celestial bodies—the Sun, Moon, and stars—of course were a help. On a clear day or night, when the Sun or Moon was visible, a navigator could always tell roughly where east and west were. In the Northern Hemisphere, the so-called Pole Star, easily visible on a clear night, told him where north was. In time, very careful charts of the movements of the stars would be made, which could be used to help navigators determine their position. There were no such charts in Columbus's time, although enough was known about certain star movements to help a little.

But of course the stars were of no use on a cloudy night. There were, however, a few basic navigational tools. The compass had been in use for centuries, although it was not well understood that magnetic north tended to wander. (Columbus would increase awareness of this tendency.) There was also the quadrant for measuring the angle of the Sun above the southern horizon. Calculating this angle could give a navigator an idea of how far north or south of the equator the ship was—in other words, determine its latitude. But there was no system for figuring out longitude, where you were east or west of a given point. That would not be developed for more than two centuries.

Generally, navigators worked by a system known as dead reckoning. Each day the navigator would toss overboard a log with a rope tied to it. By timing how long it took the rope to run out to its full length, the navigator could estimate the ship's speed. If he knew his speed and the direction he was going, the navigator could then figure out where he was in respect to where he had been the day before. If he kept careful track day by day, he would know where he was on the vast sea at any moment.

There were all sorts of problems with dead reckoning, however. For one thing, little errors could be—and usually were—introduced each day, so that after a couple of weeks the navigator might be as much as a hundred miles off. For another, a heavy storm, which could blow the ship hundred of miles off course, would destroy any idea the navigator had of where he was, leaving him to guess at the ship's location. When this happened, a ship might wander for weeks without finding land, until food and water were exhausted and the sailors died off one by one.

Yet despite all these handicaps—the hit-and-miss navigation systems, the basic understanding of the winds—Columbus again and

Navigational instruments were simple and few in Columbus's time. One valuable tool was the quadrant, which measured the angle of a celestial body—the Moon, Sun, or stars—from the horizon. The quadrant was helpful in determining how far the observer was from the equator.

again chose the right course to get where he wanted to go. It is fair to say that he had a genius for navigation. Not once in his four trips into uncharted waters did he go seriously off course.

On August 3, 1492, Columbus raised sail and set off from Palos on what would prove to be a momentous voyage. He was headed for the Canary Islands, where he could replenish his stores of food and water. Other Atlantic islands, such as the Azores and Cape Verde, were farther into the Atlantic than the Canaries, but they were controlled by Portugal. The Canaries belonged to Spain, and this was a Spanish-sponsored voyage.

An engraving by the famous Theodor de Bry. In truth, the royal couple was not present to see Columbus off on his first voyage. De Bry later made the first important European drawings of Native Americans, which gave us some idea of the people Columbus met in the New World.

By sailing to the Canaries, a trip European mariners had made many times, Columbus could start across the Atlantic with the northeast trade winds behind him. For the return trip, he could sail north for a few days and ride the westerlies blowing toward Europe. Without a doubt, he made the right choice.

The trip to the Canary Islands was quick and uneventful. He lingered in the Canaries for a bit to make needed repairs and to take on additional supplies. Then he waited for the right wind. Early in September, one began to blow. On September 6, 1492, the little fleet set sail again, heading due west.

At first things went smoothly, but days passed and no land was sighted. Columbus may have been a great navigator, but he had made that one major error—assuming that the Indies were only a few hundred miles out in the Atlantic.

The sailors began to grow uneasy: shouldn't they have sighted land by now? Columbus himself began to realize that he had been wrong. The Indies were apparently farther away than he had thought. But Columbus was a man who never doubted himself. Perhaps his calculations were off, but the Indies were certainly out there somewhere beyond the horizon.

However, in order to calm the crew, Columbus began putting down in his log distances that were considerably less than the ship had actually traveled each day. This way he hoped to convince everybody that the little fleet had not gone nearly as far as it had, and that Columbus's calculations were more or less correct.

By the first week of October, it was not only the crew that was grumbling. Martín Alonso Pinzón, owner and commander of the *Pinta*, was also raising questions. As partner in the venture, did he not have a right to some concern? According to a map Columbus had brought with him, Cipangu—Japan—lay south of their course. Pinzón began to insist that they shift their course southward.

Land looms in the distance, but not the rich realm of the Indies
Columbus had hoped to find.

Columbus, not Pinzón, had been named commander of the expedition by Spain's monarchs. Columbus objected to any change in course. By October 10, though, the sailors had had enough. They were at the point of mutiny, so Columbus wisely gave in, thinking that the change of course would give the men hope. He was, really, simply stalling for time. It was an important decision. If the fleet had stuck to the original course, it might have landed somewhere in present-day Florida.

However, the change was made, and the next morning a considerable amount of flotsam appeared—objects in the water such as tree branches, reeds, and even a stick that appeared to have a carving on it. Flocks of birds began to fly around the ship, many of them coming from the west. Tension gripped all on board. Eyes strained toward the western horizon. On the night of October 11, Columbus thought he saw a light on the horizon. Then at two in the morning on Friday, October 12, a watchman up in the rigging cried "*Tierra, tierra,*" the Spanish word for land. The world would never be the same.

The excitement aboard the three little ships was enormous. The sailors cheered and praised God for bringing them safely through. Gradually daylight broke, and the sun rose. Ahead was a beach flanked by trees. The ships anchored, and a launch carried Columbus and a party ashore. Native people—Indians, as they are often called today—came down to the beach to watch the strange spectacle. Columbus kneeled and claimed the land for the king and queen of Spain, disregarding the fact that it already belonged to the native residents.

Where, exactly, was he? Historians are not sure. Columbus named the land—an island he soon discovered—San Salvador, and many people continue to believe it was the island still known by that name. However, Columbus's description of the island could fit several in the vicinity, in the chain of islands now known as the Bahamas. It was probably either San Salvador or one of the nearby islands.

Columbus and the other Europeans had expected to see people— the inhabitants of the Indies, Cipangu, or Cathay. But they were not exactly sure what to expect. They described the people they saw as "naked"—meaning not so much that they were without clothes but that they were primitive. They seemed to lack the elements and trappings commonly associated with European society—books and writing,

Columbus falls to his knees to claim the land he had found for
the rulers of Spain. Historians are not sure exactly where the
landing occurred, except that it must have been on an island in
the Bahamas. Europeans did not think twice about claiming
already populated lands for their monarchs.

an understanding of mathematics, and technologically advanced items
such as oceangoing vessels, steel, and firearms. Most importantly, they
lacked the Christian religion. Europeans thought that God wished them

A woodcut shows Columbus giving small gifts and tokens to the
Indians after landing in the Caribbean.

to Christianize the rest of the world. It was a truth beyond argument, they believed, that only followers of Christ had a chance of going to heaven. It was, therefore, in the view of most Europeans, in the interests of native peoples to embrace Christianity. While Columbus and nearly all other Europeans believed this—as some Christians still do—it also made a good justification for forcing the native residents to come under the command of the Europeans. To the Europeans, almost anything was allowed if it brought people to the Christian religion. But the native Americans had quite different ideas about themselves, the world, and spirituality. It was inevitable that the two peoples would eventually clash.

At first, the native people seemed to Columbus to be friendly and peaceful. He was not particularly worried about them. He still thought he had landed in the Indies, which is of course why he had called the region's inhabitants Indians. He was far more interested in locating the riches that the Indies were supposed to be teeming with than he was in learning more about the people. For the next few weeks, he sailed among the islands at the eastern end of the Caribbean Sea. Eventually he came to the island now called Cuba, and then another large island, which he named Hispaniola. It is now divided between Haiti and the Dominican Republic.

Cuba, he decided, was Cipangu, or Japan. But the island lacked the luxurious goods he thought Japan would have, so he revised his initial impression. It must, instead, have been a peninsula of Cathay, or China. The Indians on the island did have some items made of gold, mostly ornaments and jewelry. So Columbus concluded that there had to be gold mines close by. Was that not what everyone expected from the Indies? In any case, gold was what everybody except for Columbus primarily wanted, what they had made their trip for. After a month, Martín Alonso Pinzón realized that they were not finding much gold. He was bored, and he was tired of taking orders from Columbus.

# THE PEOPLE COLUMBUS FOUND

Columbus of course thought he had reached the Indies and assumed that the people he met on landing in the Bahamas were Indians, a general term applied to all the native peoples he came across. Of course, the Indians did not share a single culture. In fact, Indian culture was in some respects more varied than the European one. Although Europeans spoke several dozen languages, they had one in common—Latin. It was spoken by monks, priests, and educated people in general. Agriculturally, Europeans raised the same kinds of animals for food and labor and a similar range of crops including wheat, rye, barley, and some fruits and vegetables. Europeans also shared one main religion, Roman Catholicism.

Indians, in contrast, spoke around five hundred different languages. Their cultures and economies varied enormously. In the Northwest, the people carved huge totem poles and got much of their protein from large sea creatures, including whales. In the Southwest, tribes lived mostly by growing corn. In the eastern woodlands, ranging from Canada to Virginia, the Indians cultivated gardens of corn, melons, squash, and beans; hunted deer; and harvested fish, clams, and oysters from the rivers and ocean.

These groups also had many skilled warriors among their ranks. How, then, did a tiny handful of Europeans, mostly Spanish, manage to bring these great societies under their command? The Europeans had the advantage of gunpowder-based weapons, steel swords and armor, advanced seagoing ships, and horses. In addition, the various individual Indian groups tended to be rivals. Many of them were consistently at war with one another, and the Europeans were quick to divide and conquer. Another major problem, although it did not appear immediately, was that the Indians had no natural immunity to European diseases. Within a generation of Columbus's arrival, a series of epidemics swept through various areas of the New World wiping out from 90 to 95 percent of the villages found there—just another indication of the ways native life was deeply impacted by the arrival of the Europeans and would never be the same.

So without getting permission from Columbus, he sailed away on his own to hunt for gold.

Columbus, however, had a larger dream to pursue. He was determined to found an empire under the Spanish crown with him as its ruler. He would build towns and cities and find vast wealth not only in gold but in spices, pearls, and silks. He would also bring Christianity to the people of the Indies. To simply become a gold hunter was a small thing compared to building an empire.

Many of the Indians were impressed by European guns, swords, and armor. Columbus was able to trade beads and bells he had brought from Europe for gold and, more importantly, for food for his sailors. He decided to make Hispaniola his base. There he would found the first city of his empire.

As he was making these plans, the *Santa Maria*, never a good ship to begin with, ran aground and sank. Columbus saw this as a sign, for he could use the planks from the *Santa Maria* to build a fortification, the first step on the road to empire.

Once he had completed his fort, he thought about going back to Spain. The idea was reinforced when Pinzón returned, bringing with him a good deal of gold, which he had either traded for or taken as plunder. Columbus has also collected samples of some natural products like chile, cinnamon, pineapple, and tobacco—although he did not yet know what the Indians used tobacco for. He also had two creations unknown to the Spanish, the canoe and the hammock. He would also bring with him their creators, Indians, as examples of the people he had found in the Indies.

Columbus was satisfied that he had scored a great success. He had, so he believed, shown that the Indies could be reached by sailing west. He had found gold, spices, and other previously unknown items.

Ultimately, he was deluding himself. He had not found the Indies, and the goods he was carrying back to Spain would hardly cover the cost

Columbus's flag ship, the Santa Maria, was wrecked on the rocks off Hispaniola. Columbus took this as a sign that he should start building his colony there, using the wood from the ship to make his fort.

The canoe was among the novelties Columbus witnessed in the New World. This engraving was adapted from a drawing by Theodor de Bry. It pictures Indians collecting crops for the storehouse shown behind them.

of the trip. In time Columbus's discoveries would make Spain the richest nation in Europe, if not the world. But as he made his way back to Spain in the winter of 1493, that did not appear likely.

# F O U R
# The Growing Obsession

For the trip home, Columbus headed north until he could pick up the favorable westerly winds and then set his course for Spain. Once again he had chosen correctly. Unfortunately, that winter was a rough one. The little vessels were hit by a terrible storm. He wrote:

> *The sea began to swell and the sky grew stormy. . . . We could neither advance nor make our way out of the waves attacking the caravels and breaking against them. . . . If the caravels had not been very good ships and well repaired, they would surely have been lost.*

The sailors were in a panic. They fell to their knees and prayed to be saved. Many of them made vows to make pilgrimages to holy places if they were spared a watery death. The *Pinta*, with Martín Pinzón in command, was soon separated from the *Nina*. Where had

This picture, painted about a hundred years after Columbus's time, shows a ship battling a storm. Fierce weather regularly sank European ships, usually with the loss of all life aboard.

the winds taken it? Had it sunk?

For three days, the storm continued. Then it lessened, and not long after, Columbus sighted land—the islands of the Azores, as he had expected. But there was no word of the *Pinta*.

From the Azores, Columbus headed for Lisbon. There, once people learned where he had been and what he had done, he was greeted with great astonishment.

There was still no sign of Pinzón and the *Pinta*. The other ship had already landed in a Spanish port. Pinzón prepared to travel to the court to report to Ferdinand and Isabella on the magnificent voyage. Had he arrived first, he would certainly have played up his role as Columbus's partner and would perhaps have taken much of the credit for the exploit. But before he could get to the court Pinzón died and is today forgotten to history. Did he deserve more credit? Perhaps. He, too, had faith in the voyage, and he had been important in getting the venture started. But it was Columbus's vision, his drive and persistence, that brought the plan into being; and it was his courage and navigational skills that made it work.

Inevitably, when Columbus reached the Spanish court, he made as much of the adventure as he could. He insisted that he had found the Indies and that great riches awaited Spain. Not everybody agreed. Some experts were sure that the world was larger than Columbus believed. Columbus had discovered not the Indies but altogether new lands, they said. However, Columbus had his supporters. Despite the fact that the expedition had not come back with shiploads of gold, pearls, and spices, Ferdinand and Isabella agreed that there were great possibilities in the region that Columbus had found. Within months they agreed to support another venture. This time the goal would be to establish a colony and to make further explorations, both to seek gold and to decide if the lands were the Indies or somewhere else, somewhere previously unknown.

This second voyage was to be a much bigger effort. Columbus was given seventeen ships carrying seeds for planting, sheep and horses for breeding, and 1,300 total men, including some armored cavalry.

The new fleet set off on September 25, 1493, headed for Hispaniola,

By the nineteenth century, interest in Columbus's exploits was growing. This painting, showing Columbus greeting Ferdinand and Isabella on his return from his first voyage, was made by Eugene Delacroix, one of the most famous artists of his day.

where Columbus had built his little fort during the first voyage. He took a more southerly route this time, which modern historians have confirmed to be exactly the best route for an Atlantic crossing. The fleet made landfall at the island of Dominica and proceeded northwest to what are now the Virgin Islands and Puerto Rico. This time two foolhardy Indians attacked them. The attackers were quickly captured, but it was a sign that relations between the Indians and the Spanish would not be as peaceable as Columbus had once hoped.

An early map of Columbus's settlement, which he called Isabella. Maps of the time frequently included drawings. The city shown at left is far more elaborate than anything that would be built in the New World in the decades following Columbus's voyages.

Then Columbus headed for Hispaniola to see how his fort was doing. Twenty-five miles (40.2 kilometers) from his destination, he sent a team ashore for water. They found the decaying corpses of two men tied together. One of them had a beard, which Indians did not grow. The fleet hurried on to the fort. It had been razed. The men Columbus had left behind were dead, scattered around the area for several miles.

The story of the European takeover of the Americas proved to be tragic for the people already living there. Inevitably, the question of who was to blame comes up. Obviously, if the Europeans had stayed home there would not have been a problem. That was not going to happen, for during this period Europe was becoming increasingly overpopulated. Sooner or later, Europeans would have been reaching out for new lands.

Could the Europeans have somehow managed things more peacefully? Unhappily, probably not. For one thing, people do not usually like seeing strangers coming to their lands. The Indians were no different. Some of them stole from the settlers, or even killed them when they could. Often they did not try to help the foreigners when they were short of food.

The Europeans were hardly blameless, though. They came with the idea that they were a superior people with an obligation to bring Christianity and European ways in general to the Indians. In addition, Columbus's men were not saints. They missed their families, were eager to find gold, and often short on food. Because they had firearms and swords, they could take what they wanted, sometimes killing Indians in the process.

Columbus himself wanted to stay on peaceful terms with the Indians and tried to restrain his men. But like the rest, he considered them an inferior people. He agreed to capture them for slaves and at times fought them when he felt he had to. In total, there was little hope that the exploration of the New World could have been accomplished peacefully.

A woodcut shows Columbus meeting with Indians, this time
on what would become Cuba.

Columbus was determined to extend his reputation in the New World. With that drive that was so much a part of him, he set about building a small Spanish colony on another part of Hispaniola. When he had the colony started, he set off again to look for gold. He knew that only the discovery of great riches would justify such an expensive expedition. For weeks he wandered with his ships around Cuba and Jamaica, looking for gold mines. Everywhere he went the Indians, probably to get rid of him, told him of gold that could be found always on another island. In some places, he found enough gold to keep his hopes alive. But it was not nearly as much as he had desired.

He still believed that Cuba was part of the Asian mainland. Once he came within 100 miles (161 kilometers) of the western end of the island. Had he gone farther, he would have realized that Cuba was not part of a mainland. If he had sailed even farther west, in two or three days he would have reached Mexico, where a fortune in gold awaited later explorers. But he pursued none of these courses and thus did not find what he was seeking—the rich people of Cathay and Cipangu he was sure were residing somewhere in these lands. So he turned back.

He had now been gone for almost two years. Some of his ships had returned to Spain to collect provisions. Some of the people on these ships reported that Columbus was not managing affairs well and that little gold had been found. Ferdinand and Isabella sent an official out to investigate. He arrived in Hispaniola in October 1495. Disagreements between Columbus and the official ensued. Columbus began to see that back in Spain people were openly criticizing him to the monarchs. Still, he had not accomplished what he had set out to do. But he believed that in simply holding the colony together in the face of hostile Indians and undisciplined men—much less cultivating crops unsuited to the Caribbean—he had done much. He decided he had better go home, with his head held high, and defend himself.

A nineteenth-century view of Ferdinand and Isabella
meeting with Columbus. Despite lingering doubts, the cautious
couple still supported their ambitious explorer.

He reached Spain in June 1496. He was able to persuade the monarchs that he had been their faithful servant and that the hope for wealth from the Indies was still good. The tough-minded Ferdinand and Isabella had their doubts about Columbus's ability to manage a colony, but they still have much faith in him.

Columbus could simply have quit. He had a noble life, and his share of the wealth coming out of the lands he had found was growing. He would in time be rich. But he remained obsessed. He was determined to achieve the greatness he felt he deserved. So he spent the next two years reading reports from Hispaniola and preparing for yet another trip.

Meanwhile, news of the discoveries had spread. Europe was excited by tales of this amazing new land that only a few years earlier nobody even knew of. Other monarchs, hearing of the gold found in these distant lands, began making plans. In 1497 the English king Henry VII sent an Italian sea captain named Giovanni Caboto, known today as John Cabot, across the North Atlantic. He probably landed at Cape Breton, part of Nova Scotia in present-day Canada. Like Columbus, Cabot thought he had found China.

In the same year, the Portuguese sent Vasco da Gama to find a route to India. He went around the southern tip of Africa and in 1498 reached Calicut, a city in western India. In so doing, he accomplished what Columbus had hoped to do—find the wealth of the Indies. In 1497 an Italian adventurer named Amerigo Vespucci made the first of several

The Portuguese were the first Europeans to make important explorations, especially along the African coast. This Portuguese stamp from 1969 shows Vasco da Gama, who sailed around the southern tip of Africa and in 1498 reached India. It was da Gama, thus, and not Columbus, who discovered the best route to the East.

voyages to the new lands, although historians disagree over exactly what he did and where he went. In 1499 a Spanish rival to Columbus, Alonso de Hojeda, who had been on Columbus's second trip, came to the Caribbean searching for riches. The game was slipping from Columbus's hands.

To him, all these other adventurers were meddlers, taking advantage of a trail he had blazed. The new lands, he believed, had been discovered by him and were his, given to him by the Spanish monarchs. However it went beyond human rulers: Columbus still saw himself as an agent of God who had been specifically selected for this great task. What business did these other people have interfering with his God-given work? So in 1498 he set off again.

This time he took an even more southerly route, hoping to come across a huge continent that was rumored to be in the South Atlantic. This was, of course, South America. By chance, he found it. On July 31, 1498, he sighted the island of Trinidad, which is just off the coast of Venezuela. He sailed the short distance to the mainland, traveling along what is now the peninsula of Paria. In his log he wrote that he had discovered "a very great continent, which until today had been unknown." On that account, he was right.

But after this promising start, things grew worse. The colony he had founded in Hispaniola was still thriving, but some of the men were in revolt against his authority. Columbus put down the rebellion and re-established control. But, at the same time, new expeditions from Spain were arriving in Hispaniola. Columbus was enraged at these intrusions. In addition, back at the court some people were again attacking Columbus for their own reasons.

The monarchs once more decided to send an official to Hispaniola to investigate. He and Columbus were suspicious of each other from the start. The official had been given orders to take over if he felt that Columbus was mismanaging the colony. Ultimately, he decided Columbus was.

He had Columbus arrested and sent him back to Spain in chains. The Admiral of the Ocean Sea was now nothing but a common prisoner.

On the trip home, the captain of the ship offered to take the chains off, but Columbus proudly insisted on wearing them. In chains he was brought before Ferdinand and Isabella. They instantly freed him and once again assured him of their support.

But for Columbus, his life of adventure was winding down. He was fifty, which was relatively old for that time. He health was gradually deteriorating. His spirits were drooping. He believed that he had performed a great task and was being cheated of his rewards. More and more, he was living in a world of illusion.

Incredibly, Columbus would not give up. In May 1502 he left Spain once more, heading across the Atlantic, still hoping to find the remarkable wealth of the Indies. He believed that what we today call South America was a great new continent, ripe for new discoveries. But he still clung to the belief that the lands farther north in the Caribbean were the Indies, which he also had found the route to.

This time he pushed across the Caribbean, where he expected he would find Japan or China. By July he was sailing along the Central American coast from what is now Honduras to Panama. He thus became the first European to cross the Caribbean and reach Central America.

Marco Polo, in his reports on the Indies, talked about an isthmus, with a strait, or water passage, running along it and into a great ocean. This was the Malay Peninsula, with its strait leading into the Indian Ocean. Columbus concluded that he was sailing along one side of Marco Polo's isthmus. If he could find the strait through or around it, he would have at last discovered passage to the Indies.

Columbus was right on two points. He was indeed traveling along an isthmus—the isthmus of Panama, through which the Panama Canal would be dug some four hundred years later. Second, beyond it was a great ocean—the Pacific. But he was wrong on the key points. There

An artist's version of Columbus being brought back to
Europe in chains.

was no strait through it, and if there had been, the Indies were still
thousands of miles to the west.

Once again, Columbus missed an opportunity. By looking for something that was not there, he missed what was there. If he had continued
to travel north and west he would have reached Mexico and the outskirts
of the Aztec empire, which would have brought a fortune to Spain.

Soon, though, disaster tumbled in on him. His ships began to leak.

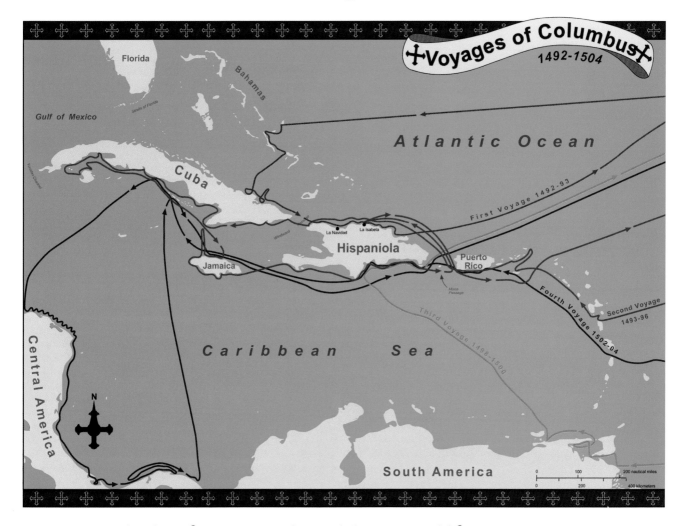

Columbus's four voyages changed the New World forever. Europeans would quickly establish their presence there.

Storms blew him out to sea, and eventually he was marooned on Jamaica. Only by luck did he make it back to Hispaniola, and in September 1504, he sailed back to Spain. His health and his spirits were broken. Wealthy from his share of the profits from the Spanish colonies, more and more, he lived in his dreams and relished his past glories. On May 20, 1506, he died. Fifty years later, he was virtually forgotten.

# FIVE

# What Did Columbus Really Do?

Christopher Columbus did not discover America. The first humans in the Western Hemisphere arrived there at least 20,000 years earlier and, according to some historians, possibly even before. These were people who crossed from Siberia into Alaska and spread throughout the New World from there. Their descendants were, of course, the Indians who Columbus found when he explored the islands of the Caribbean.

Columbus was not even the first European to access the New World. Vikings from Scandinavia, great seamen, frequently visited both Iceland and Greenland and built colonies there. Historians generally believe that they eventually came to Newfoundland and even tried to build a colony there before they were pushed out by the Indians. There are myths and rumors about others who found their way to the New

A detail of a portrait of Columbus. It is probably not a very good likeness. Because we know so little about the great explorer, painters were forced to invent their own vision of him.

World—sailors lost at sea who were cast up by chance in South America. And there are those who think that the Chinese may have reached South America long before Columbus did.

Ultimately, none of these early discoveries resulted in much. By Columbus's time, the Viking trips had been forgotten, and if any others had found the New World by chance, there was no evidence of it.

It was Columbus who opened the way for Europeans who so quickly followed. It was he, and not anyone else, who had the inner drive, the intelligence, and the determination to see it through. He dreamed of greatness and would not give up until he found it. He was a risk taker, a defier of odds. Others around him argued endlessly about the size of the Earth, the distance to the Indies, and other unknown quantities. Columbus created the opportunity and set out on his voyages of discovery, while others simply talked and debated.

Columbus made many mistakes, but despite everything, he did the important things right. He had a natural instinct for navigation and kept his ships going through storms and strife. In the end, he knew as much about the seas as anyone. Among other things, he contributed much to our understanding of the Atlantic wind patterns. He was the first European to sight the American mainland, the first to cross the Caribbean, and the first to reach Central America. Perhaps most important, he brought home enough gold and other goods to encourage Europeans to go out and look for more.

That of itself was a matter of huge importance, for it drew other Europeans to follow the course Columbus had marked out. Within a generation the Spanish and Portuguese, in particular, were building colonies in the New World. Soon they would be joined by the English, the French, the Dutch, and others. And the world was changed forever.

Why, then, is America not called Columbia? It has to do with Amerigo Vespucci. He was from Florence, Italy, and worked for a bank in Seville. He made several trips to the New World in the wake of

Amerigo Vespucci, following in Columbus's footsteps, made several trips to the New World. His description of his journeys was widely circulated, and people came to believe that he had discovered America. Columbus was soon almost forgotten.

Columbus's discoveries. Vespucci was "a very fast and zealous self-promoter," according to one historian. Some years after Columbus's voyages, Vespucci wrote a description of his own trips. This report was widely circulated, and it led people to believe that Vespucci, not Columbus, had discovered the new lands. Soon somebody suggested that the land ought to be called America. By this time, Columbus was dead. His heirs did not take up the fight for him, and soon Columbus was all but forgotten.

Then, in the late eighteenth century, almost three hundred years after the first voyage, people began to rediscover Columbus. Fame began to find him again. After the American Revolution, King's College in New York City changed its name to Columbia College. When the capital of the new nation was set up, the city was named for George Washington and the district for Christopher Columbus.

Inevitably, it was Americans who were most interested in finding out the truth. In 1828 the celebrated author Washington Irving published a biography of Columbus. Soon the Spanish government ordered an investigation. What remained of the original documents left by Columbus and others was pulled together. Scholars set to work, and within a few decades Columbus finally got justice. In 1892 the four hundredth anniversary of the famous crossing was celebrated throughout Europe and America. The five hundredth anniversary of the trip, which came in 1992, was also widely celebrated, but this time amid controversy. Some people felt that Columbus ought to be seen as one of the Europeans who exploited the Native Americans who had in fact "discovered" America themselves long before. They did not feel that he ought to be seen as a hero. But even so, most Americans joined in the celebrations and continue to, marking the day with parades and special events. Besides a famous university and our nation's capital, there is a river named for him and at least two dozen cities and towns. There are many placed named Columbia in Canada, in particular the

Perceptions of Columbus began to change in the nineteenth century. Today he is one of the most celebrated of American heroes. Columbus Day is a national holiday. Here a marching band gets ready for a parade to mark the occasion in New York City in 2002.

province of British Columbia. In South America, an entire nation pays homage with its name—Colombia.

So in the end Columbus got his due, perhaps even more than he expected, for he is certainly one of the best-known people in history.

# CHRISTOPHER COLUMBUS AND HIS TIMES

1451    Christopher Columbus is born in Genoa in what will become Italy.

1476    He moves to Lisbon, Portugal.

1484    The king of Portugal fails to back Columbus's plan to find a faster route to the East.

1486    Columbus moves to Castile to gain greater access to the Spanish court.

1492    Ferdinand and Isabella grant Columbus the money he needs to get his expedition under way.

August    He leaves Spain in August.

October    Land is sighted in the New World.
Columbus arrives in what is today Cuba.

December The *Santa Maria* sinks off the coast of Hispaniola.
Columbus uses the wood from the ship to build a fortification.

1493    Columbus returns to Europe.
He embarks on his second voyage.

1496    He returns to Europe once again.

1498    Columbus leaves on his third voyage.

1500    He is arrested for mismanaging the colony and sent back to Europe in chains.

1502   He makes his fourth and final voyage.

1504   Columbus returns home.

1506   He dies on May 20.

# Further Research

## Books

For Teachers

Fernández-Armesto, Felipe. *Columbus.* New York: Oxford University Press, 1991.

Granzotto, Gianni. *Christopher Columbus: The Dream and the Obsession.* New York: Doubleday, 1985.


For Students

Brenner, Barbara. *If You Were There in 1492: Everyday Life in the Time of Columbus.* New York: Aladdin, 1998.

Kudlinski, Kathleen. *Christopher Columbus: Young Explorer.* New York: Aladdin, 2005.

Meltzer, Milton. *Columbus and the World around Him.* Danbury, CT: Franklin Watts, 1991.

Pelta, Kathy. *Discovering Christopher Columbus: How History Is Invented.* Minneapolis: Lerner, 1991.

Roop, Peter and Connie, eds. *In Their Own Words: Christopher Columbus.* New York: Scholastic, 2001.


## Web Sites

1492: An Ongoing Voyage

http://www.ibiblio.org/expo/1492.exhibit/Intro.html


Christopher Columbus: Explorer

http://www.enchantedlearning.com/explorers/page/c/columbus.shtml

# Further Research

The Columbus Navigation Homepage

http://www1.minn.net/~keithp/

Discovery Channel: Columbus—Secrets from the Grave

http://dsc.discovery.com/convergence/columbus/columbus.html

The Eastern Voyages of Exploration

http://www.ucalgary.ca/applied_history/tutor/eurvoya/columbus.html

The Mariners' Museum: Christopher Columbus

http://www.mariner.org/educationalad/ageofex/columbus.php

The Round Earth and Christopher Columbus

http://www-spof.gsfc.nasa.gov/stargaze/Scolumb.htm

# Index

Page numbers in **boldface** are illustrations.

79